By Word of Mouth
The Poetry of Dennis Cooley

By Word of Mouth
The Poetry of Dennis Cooley

Selected
with an
introduction by
Nicole Markotić
and an
afterword by
Dennis Cooley

lps
LAURIER POETRY SERIES

Wilfrid Laurier University Press
[WLU]

We acknowledge the support of the Canada Council for the Arts for our publishing program. We acknowledge the financial support of the Government of Canada through the Book Publishing Industry Development Program for our publishing activities.

Library and Archives Canada Cataloguing in Publication

Cooley, Dennis, 1944–

By word of mouth : the poetry of Dennis Cooley / selected, with an introduction by Nicole Markotić; and an afterword by Dennis Cooley.

(Laurier poetry series)
Includes bibliographical references.
ISBN-13: 978-1-55458-007-1

I. Markotić, Nicole II. Title. III. Series.

PS8555.O575B92 2007   C811'.54   C2007-901766-5

© 2007 Wilfrid Laurier University Press
Waterloo, Ontario, Canada N2L 3C5
www.wlupress.wlu.ca

Cover photograph © 2007 by R.W. Harwood. Cover and text design by P.J. Woodland.

Every reasonable effort has been made to acquire permission for copyright material used in this text, and to acknowledge all such indebtedness accurately. Any errors and omissions called to the publisher's attention will be corrected in future printings.

This book is printed on 100% post-consumer recycled paper.

Printed in Canada

Table of Contents

Foreword

At the beginning of the twenty-first century, poetry in Canada—writing and
publishing it, reading and thinking about it—finds itself in a strangely con-
flicted place. We have many strong poets continuing to produce exciting new
work, and there is still a small audience for poetry; but increasingly, poetry
is becoming a vulnerable art, for reasons that don't need to be rehearsed.

But there are things to be done: we need more real engagement with our
poets. There needs to be more access to their work in more venues—in class-
rooms, in the public arena, in the media—and there needs to be more, and
more different kinds of publications, that make the wide range of our con-
temporary poetry more widely available.

The hope that animates this new series from Wilfrid Laurier University
Press is that these volumes will help to create and sustain the larger reader-
ship that contemporary Canadian poetry so richly deserves. Like our fiction
writers, our poets are much celebrated abroad; they should just as properly
be better known at home.

Our idea has been to ask a critic (sometimes herself a poet) to select thirty-
five poems from across a poet's career; write an engaging, accessible introduc-
tion; and have the poet write an afterword. In this way, we think that the usual
practice of teaching a poet through eight or twelve poems from an anthology
will be much improved upon; and readers in and out of classrooms will have
more useful, engaging, and comprehensive introductions to a poet's work.
Readers might also come to see more readily, we hope, the connections
among, as well as the distances between, the life and the work.

It was the ending of an Al Purdy poem that gave Margaret Laurence the
epigraph for *The Diviners*: "but they had their being once/and left a place
to stand on." Our poets still do, and they are leaving many places to stand on.
We hope that this series will help, variously, to show how and why this is so.

—*Neil Besner*
General Editor

Biographical Note

Dennis Cooley's poetry has been influenced by William Carlos Williams, H.D., Robert Duncan, Charles Olson, and e.e. cummings. As well, the prairies and Canadian poets such as Eli Mandel, Andrew Suknaski, Daphne Marlatt, bpNichol, Michael Ondaatje, and Robert Kroetsch have shaped and inspired his poems and poetics. Roaming the page, Cooley insists on disturbing the formal poetic inheritance he both esteems and from which he breaks away. Born in Estevan, Saskatchewan, on August 27, 1944, Dennis Cooley grew up in Saskatchewan and currently lives, teaches, and writes in Winnipeg, Manitoba. He is married to Diane, and father of two daughters, Megan and Dana. He has written close to a dozen books of poetry, one literary travel book, a book of essays, and has edited five books. Dennis Cooley has published widely in Canadian literary journals, helped to establish the Manitoba Writers Guild, and was a founding editor of Turnstone Press. A 1998 issue of *Prairie Fire* dedicated an entire issue to Dennis Cooley's writing, revealing his passion for writing, reading, teaching, literary dialogue, and his keen engagement with the world around him. His books take on historical and fictional characters— while never entirely curving into narrative—in order to recount the less-heard stories of the underprivileged and the unfamiliar. Writing becomes political when you play with "certain kinds of voices that might enter and might become honoured in a literary world," Cooley says in *Prairie Fire*. That engagement with—and ambiguity of—speaking voices invites readers to question authority, to challenge institutionalized privilege. Again and again, Dennis Cooley returns to the prairie vernacular—not to reflect, but to play: "I want reference and I want syntactical surprise and breakage and crazy puns and syllables freed loose and I want emotion and I want parody." Dennis Cooley earned a Bachelor of Education, a Bachelor of Arts, and a Master of Arts from the University of Saskatchewan, as well as a PhD from the University of Rochester, SUNY. He is a professor at St. John's College at the University of Manitoba, where he continues to write and to inspire students with his playful love of language.

Introduction

By Word of Mouth: An Introduction to Dennis Cooley's Poetry[1]

> "Cuz it's always gotta be blood."
> —Spike, *Buffy the Vampire Slayer*

More and more, when teaching poetry, I find myself defending difficult poetics, those unique and complicated aspects of language that encourage readers to believe in the White Queen's "six impossible things before breakfast" (Carroll 101).[2] I accept that students (especially with a final exam approaching) want to know that they know what they know. But as Dennis Cooley remarks in a 1987 essay on the line break: "formal departure disturbs readers" ("Breaking and Entering" 79); indeed, departure from inherited forms does nudge readers to stray from their chosen comfort zone, to try, at least, to believe one or two impossible things, perhaps by lunchtime. So what—or where—is it, exactly, towards which this poet nudges readers? Poetry, says Dennis Cooley, "becomes vigorously rooted—in *our* time and in *our* place" (*The Vernacular Muse* 182). That the "our" changes as constantly as the times and the places proves his point that the Canadian canon is ever versatile, ever affected by its involved readership. Our place, our bodies, our language.

By not simply writing poetry directed towards what modernist poet Laura Riding calls the "plain reader" (Riding 218), Dennis Cooley changes and changes the rules, shifting *all* his readers towards an engagement with poetry as an act of capricious rebellion: through excessive attention to the line break, or to a word, or by sowing words across margins. "One of the consequences of scattering words on the page," says Cooley, "or not offering a certain kind of pact through a text, is that it will give your readers a lot of permission but it also puts a lot of pressure on them" (*Prairie Fire* 49). Dennis Cooley flirts with the reader, teases the reader, invites his readers to share in the fun.

For Cooley, innovation means breaking away from established literary conventions, or traditions. Stuttering, stumbling, sprinkling a plethora of line indents and breaks, tripping over confining institutions, ruled corridors, imprisoned language, barred windows, falling out and falling away, fracturing the old, landing prairie-flat on his face, hesitating, hobbling through the ruptures, limping towards a new rhythm.

now our blood stirs
     at this curve's list
this slug
        slung in
                gorging weight. (*Leaving* 7)

The poem doesn't fracture so much as it engorges: collapses and swells, curves
the line with little regard for the metred, measured stanza, for verse conven-
tions, or the crescendo enjambment (the body jammed up, the body's limbs
striding forward and returning, the poem's lines kissing and parting and
kissing again). But "falling away" from poetic conventions doesn't mean the
poet has abandoned standards or principles or even poetic customs. Here,
for example, is what Cooley asks of contemporary verse: "what has been
happening to poetry that it should have been brought to such a state—past
metre, past rhyme, and (here's the crux) largely past metaphor and gram-
matical phrasing" ("Breaking and Entering" 79). Here's the "crux": how do
strategies of writing make room for a poet such as Dennis Cooley to challenge
conventional wisdoms, to write against the power of the norm, to *break* with
potent tradition? To bleed words all over the page? To defy sanguinity, yet
refuse sanguinarity as he delivers the poem? And how, asks Dennis Cooley,
do we recognize its bloody afterbirth?

Sociologist Pierre Bourdieu has examined the claims of mid-nineteenth-
century Parisian artists and poets who insist they invert the dominant eco-
nomic and cultural values of the bourgeoisie. His assessment has not been
favourable, pointing out that such inversions merely reinstate the hierarchy,
though tipped, now, in favour of art and decadence over upper-class refine-
ment and status. But rather than the wild Bakhtinian carnival that reinstates
the father/king at the very moment that it crowns the jester/son, Cooley looks
to less venerated classes for heroes: to Jack Krafchenko, an immigrant and a
criminal; to Irene, a mother and a woman with cancer; to Dracula, and to
Sinclair Ross's Bentleys, literary characters whose fictional lives plague poetry.
Cooley writes of loss and mourning, of astronauts and poor self-trapped
Mrs. Bentley. And all the while, this poet is consistently willing to make mis-
takes, to embrace them, even. To cultivate flaws until the flaws themselves
generate novel lines, invigorated stanzas, the embodied codex. In Cooley's
books, bodily sensations of place and belonging, of speech and reply are such
that when, for example, he writes *this only home*, he expands, as Deborah
Keahey says, his sense of place from prairie to planet (Keahey 89), not to
obliterate one with the other, but to expand the dialogue, spatially and
organically showing the cosmos as a growing garden. Upon return, an astro-

naut, risking thresholds, feels one ear as "a shoe / full of blood" ("inner ear" 66), ever listening.

The "flaw" in the poetry is not a mistake or a defect, but a literary fault line, a poetic blemish that marks the poet's shift from one formal endeavour to another. Notions of boundary crossings, and the ensuing rift, appear again and again in Dennis Cooley's oeuvre (for example, *Bloody Jack* has been read as a long poem and as a novel, *passwords* as travel writing and as poetic diary). Cooley's poems innovatively scramble over and across and around linguistic, poetic, and manuscript borders, dripping a flamboyant and crimson-red onto the lines, between the lines, with surprising scarlet stains that might appear as errors or flaws to those who don't recognize their tarnished brilliance. Commenting on the notion of critical excess in composing poetry, Charles Bernstein writes that "poetics must necessarily involve error," suggesting that poetry theory, poetry writing, and fortuitous chance come together on the page. This error, he says, comes in the form of "wandering, errantry," but also through "mistake, misperception, incorrectness, contradiction." For Cooley, such chance or contradictory writing may be a plethora of puns (such as the lines in "a poem for the other wise": "they / wont let go / of the line" and "they know exactly / where to draw / the line"[36]) or a literal text dispersal in front of the reader's eyes (many of Cooley's poems make full use of spaces and tabs across the page, but see especially the poems in *Fielding*). Error, humorously, "slips, slides … as part of the process" (Bernstein 153). Cooley is always breaking / bending / sliding / rupturing the rules, smearing the neat line between the "mother tongue / we learn / to speak" and slipping readers into and past those words we "dare not / breathe" (*Irene* 14–15). Cooley's acute formal innovation asks readers to question inherited assumptions about the inherited structures of poetry and the privileged inclusion such structures assume. He invites readers to cross a myriad of poetic borders; we Cooley readers joyfully acquiesce. The frenetic madness of the page is a roller-coaster ride, a poetry amusement park, and each word leads to the next line break twist, the next genre shout.

In his article on genre limitations and insubordination, literary critic Jacques Derrida writes of the potential for genre to exceed its boundaries, as individual members of a particular genre always signal boundary limits and excesses. Derrida explores the "laws" of genre, the rules that poets such as Dennis Cooley invoke and tease and respect and break. So that any critic's (or writer's, or even reader's) decision that a particular text does or does not fit into a particular genre is nothing more than a legislation of inclusion and exclusion: that which identifies a text within a genre, identifies the cultivation of that same genre. So that "members" of a genre re-inscribe the very categories within which they have been located. "The trait common to these classes," says Derrida, "is precisely the identifiable recurrence of a common trait by which one recognizes, or should recognize, a membership in a class" (Derrida 228).

To disrespect genre norms, to cross over the line of demarcation, pushes the writer into the realm of generic badlands. And thus genre crossings, coupled with stylistic crossings, by their very existence compel both poet and readers to confront social constructions that include nationality, gender, race, class, sexuality, and age. Such identity categories reflect hierarchical oppositions, such as good/bad or haute/lowbrow, that drive so-called master narratives. The idea of nation especially invests in and endorses oppositional binaries, insisting on division as not only between sides, but as dividing the "top/superior" from the "bottom/inferior."[3] Dennis Cooley, however, considers the implications of literary, national, and familial borders from a multiplicity of angles. Although each ensuing book of Cooley's takes on a new and exciting focus, each book also gives away the password, the secret entry, to anyone excluded, and bloody well rejoices in the outlaws whose excessive, scandalous, and outrageous behaviour resurrects us all. The poem "in his tangerine skin" from *Bloody Jack* offers, at first glance, a normative left-justified poem, with a generative narrative:

> we buried him
> in mint condition
> on his eyes
> two georges
> they shone like hens eyes
> he inhaled the dark
> *hhhhgg hhggg*
> engorged it
> like a badger breathing
> for blood
> when we shovelled him in
> christ he was a gorgeous man
> the eyes were breathing
> & shining blood

Gradually, the reader *sees* the play—the coins on the dead man's eyes, the "mint condition" that claims an economic hold on the culture of death, the "*hhhgg hhggg*" that breathes through the poem, the first-person plural pronoun that initiates the piece—each element contributes a stylistic prank to subvert conventional readings that will limit this poem to one only about the act of burial, only about a body decomposing. Why does the poet stop to remark about the beautiful corpse? How is it that the lifeless body watches them still? The sound of the dead man's inhalation, to the eyes blatantly "breathing / & shining blood" (7) undercuts the history of that dead convict securely buried, safely tucked away. Jack Krafchenko's body goes on breathing blood, until the burglarizing poet resurrects his spirit seventy years later.

Given its dependency on circulatory red corpuscles, is *Bloody Jack*, then, a precursor of the Dracula poems? Does the prairie romance of *Perishable Light* lead to the migratory transience of *passwords*? Do the local love stories of *country music* and *Dedications* invent a celestial route towards *this only home*? Does the wistful nostalgia of *Leaving* bestow the poet-voice with a language of mourning he visits in both *Fielding* and *Irene*? Do *seeing red* and *Burglar of Blood* reiterate each other's hemophiliac flow? The books bump and stroke each other, invent and initiate the next poem on the next page. Dennis Cooley has written many diverse books of poetry, yet his words return, again and again, to the body, to the notion of the body—breathing, singing, mourning, coupling, thinking, punning, bleeding, healing. Douglas Barbour, in his introduction to the "revised" edition of *Bloody Jack*, talks about satire and how it is necessarily "directed against" (ix). Calling the book "terrifying energy and savage delight" (vii), Barbour commends Cooley for changing the poems, adding new ones, exchanging a few lines, making sure, in this pre-published permanent text, that "nothing stays fixed" (xii). A book about the feisty and heroic outlaw, *Bloody Jack*, then, leads into a collection of poems that search mind (soul) / body (corporeal) connections: *Soul Searching*. A book that pays poetic tribute to his fellow writers, *Dedications*, begins to release and propel the Cooley-pun in *Perishable Light*. And the poem series giving voice to astronauts and their views of the earth, *this only home*, slips readers from the too-distant tangible world right back to the beat-beat of blood coursing through veins in *burglar of blood*. And so it goes: Dracula channels readers into the fairy tales of *goldfinger*, goldilocks suggests the enigmatic travel writing of *passwords*, a trip to Germany suggests the sunny mysteries of *sunfall*, which leads to poems tributing Sinclair Ross, and more vampires, and the poet's mother, and small-press chapbooks along the way that all fit each other (if "fit" is ever the correct description of a Cooley poem), even as they bleed into each other and on each other, and even bleed *for* each other.

Poet and critic Michael Davidson, in his essay "Strange Blood," talks about the cultural constituencies bounded by racial or national characteristics (41). Those bonds announce themselves not only through the terminology of "blood relatives," but also through phrases such as "blood brothers," "the blood line," "blood lust," and even "one drop of blood."[4] By combining his interest in a literary figure and his passion for secular scripture (the body's text, the body as text), Cooley—the master of puns, the emperor of witticisms—retools the tools of the body, the sovereignty of blood, the degeneracy of bloodlines.

> i make quite an impression
> i know that
> there's no denying
> the way I hit you
> sudden
> get a word in
> blood clot you can feel
> me beating
> breathing
> deep in your heart   (*Burglar of Blood* 31)

Dracula, in this poem, hits his victim hard and fast, before language can sort the act, before thinking can arrest the violence. The blood clot that "you" feel is the one that stops your heart, that changes you from person into the blood-sucking monster Dracula inhales through your body. Dracula, says Michael Davidson, "marks an anxiety over 'foreign' or 'ethnic' insemination into Christian life" (Davidson 45). Although Davidson is concerned, throughout his essay, with literature that presents miscegenation as pollution and corruption, I am interested in his questioning of "blood as a marker of national identity" (Davidson 51), especially as his discussion leads me to look at how Cooley recognizes that blood itself often serves as a marker of social and cultural belonging and, in the example of Dracula, of a literal corporeal shift from one "cultural" identity into another.

Dennis Cooley's chapbook *Burglar of Blood* and his recent book *seeing red* both delve into the literary history of Dracula and vampire stories as a strategy to reinvestigate the assumptions contemporary readers make about bodies, and especially the division between the outside and the inside. When Count Dracula puts his mouth onto your neck to drink, his body is inside your body, transforming your blood into his blood. As Davidson has pointed out, the image of the vampire has always disturbed gender hierarchies, as penetration is multivalent and does not necessarily behave heterosexually.[5] In fact, as contemporary fascination with vampires attests, vampires don't behave at all. Cooley, in his poems, does not attempt to redeem the pale aristocrat—to save him from the vengeful villagers—so much as to redeem the act of misbehaving, attempting to penetrate the masculine poem with the masculine line break, or the masculine poem with the feminine word.

> yes the sweet red
> river sweet as straw
> berry we build cities beside
> marry the unmanageable blood
>
> all the blood
> the whole story
> the whole bloody thing
>
> all of it, singing
> the woods ringing
> menstrual   −minstrel
>
> (*burglar of blood* 15)

In these lines, Cooley plays with the concept of the vampire's influence on his victims' bodies. Here, rather than a monster who steals heartbeats, Dracula sings a sweet ode to the feminine blood that he respects, that he understands ministers to his lover's lust for his lust, their mutual licking and swallowing of each other's juices. Cooley brilliantly plays with ideas of the "body" of language, altering readers' perception of the ravenous lover, the diabolical sinner, the naïve prey. This combination of sexuality and punning disturbs the known order as much as it heightens reading pleasure, the pleasure of wending the length of the "labiarinth" (*Dedications* 19).

A further pleasure in Cooley poetry is the oft-displayed secular faith he invokes as a rubric for rewriting the "official" story. Cooley's poetry questions when belief itself acts as interference to thinking. In *Soul Searching*, he writes, "souls were sneezes / that snooze in dough of bodies," and sinners "slept in bodies / like CO_2 cartridges" ("Paul Sd" 19). That "snooze" operates as both comical past tense for the sneeze of the soul, but also as the quick nap of the nascent soul, awaiting a corporeal "cartridge" into which it might tunnel. By challenging all poetic creeds and structural principles, Cooley rummages around the notion of spirituality:

> in fall the fields of flax
> from the mouth of night
> spun over
> night into gold
>
> & the sky & the wind
> & the spirits spurt ("Exorcism" 21)

As his language rummages around the page, readers discover that the spirit is not only secular but vernacular, materializing not only from scriptures but out of local dialect. *Soul Searching* is not so much a treatise of the persona "searching" for the psyche or essence of poetry as it is the poet/linguist's investigation into how Cartesian notions of the mind/body split have led to a sensual/spiritual tear. The body: agitated and agitating.

When, asks Cooley, is faith a leap from one page to the next? According to Smaro Kamboureli, "*Bloody Jack* is about the poet's dream of living in the margins: the lover and poet as outlaw" (Kamboureli 18). Jack Krafchenko is the criminal outlaw of the text, and thus the romantic hero in a stock western tale. But critics can never fit *Bloody Jack* into the standard tales; its male lead— by poetic classification—can also be read as a textual outlaw of liminal space. In "the love song of j l krafchenko or the trans Canada in (trance crypt," the lines wilfully ignore the page break, chasing tracks across the book's gutter, coupling across forbidden borders. The body of the poem exceeds its textual spine, its corporeal frame. "*Bloody Jack* as a book explodes its frame by displaying its anatomy" (Kamboureli 20). The book closes with an appendix that splays out beyond its first publication,[6] confronting the limits of both "poem" and "book."

The dynamic tension between the sacred and the vernacular is an attractive trope for Cooley. He names his collection of essays on the sight and sound of poems, *The Vernacular Muse*, signalling an intertwining of the Western tradition and influence on contemporary poetry, as well as the extraordinary sway of the colloquial. Into this anxious embrace Dennis Cooley delivers *Bloody Jack*. Part poetry collection, part narrative, part journalistic investigation, part parody, part parts—this poetic tale about one particular man living within a prairie landscape "earmarked" for inventory (*The Vernacular Muse* 168) gets under the reader's skin, clots and pulses and gluts into a veritable lettered nosebleed. A tongue-bleed. An idiom-bleed. A prose-bleed. A word-of-mouth hemophilia. "I myself am often not sure whose voice speaks" (12–13), Cooley pleasurably admits in an interview with Michael Bonar, indicating not only the blur between author and persona and character, but also between reader and writer, between—in this created oral poetry world—the speaker and listener.

In what I like to call a novel—because *Bloody Jack* is, still, novel to the literature of Canada's reading public and the narration of our own history— Dennis Cooley madly hails the long poem tradition in Canadian poetry, plays tribute to contemporaneous poets, such as Michael Ondaatje[7] and Robert Kroetsch.[8] He celebrates the "rhetorical" (the textual, but not literal) place that is the western Canadian prairies (*The Vernacular Muse* 5) and its not-so-rhetorical winters, singing tribute to both in his books from *Leaving* and *sunfall*. Cooley interjects letters and newspaper articles and fake appendices, and handwritten scrawl. His personas chastise detracting readers (Dracula writes a reply to his critics, chastising them for valuing only the refined and the delicate, and discounting the rough and robust), rhyme ("hey / diddle / fiddle / the / rat / and / the / riddle," in *this only home* 38), speak from the grave and rob graves, and howl at the moon ("a leprous forehead ... an eye staring thru the curtain ... a wart on an angels neck ... a cancerous lung ... an earlobe   packed with fat and hyperbole ...," in *Perishable Light* 38–41). Cooley's personas embody particular and specific words and phrases and puns and images—their bodies interacting and responding to the world.

Dennis Cooley, the coulee-bred cooliest poet who cannot refuse a pun, must re-fuse the poetic line, the metric stanza, the conked-out metaphor: "i am therefore i anapest," he declaims, "poems should be sprayed with ana-pesticide" ("Breaking and Entering" 94). Robert Kroetsch, writing on the line as horizon, says that Dennis Cooley believes the prairies are, "literally, a series of puns" (Kroetsch 211). So often, when reading Cooley poems, snorts erupt from the reader's throat, from he/r belly. Rolling one's eyes is as much a response to the Cooley-pun as hoots and giggles, but Cooley can also cause the reader's lungs a sudden intake of air because his wordplay is so off-kilter, so on-target, that the reading body physically acknowledges its precision, as, for example, in *country music*, when the poet advises:

> face it my friends
> our days are leased
> now & then released"
>
> ...
>
> what can I say
> that's the way things go
>
> ....
>
> way to go
> is what you should say

These stanzas are rowdy yet precise; their format holds each image carefully, and circulates the words so as to tempt the next line, the next retort, the next cooley-ish comeback. Conversely, in Cooley's books about his parents' deaths, such fooling around can express exuberance, but also allows poet and readers to access the fragmentation of grief:

> & we are skinbags of heated water   dreaming
> brains grayly

```
                    balloon in our heads
                                    nerves skein     blind
                                  albino seaweed blown
                  in our bodies' pools
                                    listening
                                        (Fielding unpaginated)
```

    Although Cooley's poems about grief and loss are not restricted to his
books *Fielding* (which narrates the death of his father) and *Irene* (which
explores the connections he understands—and those he doesn't—to his
mother), these two texts allow readers to observe the punning Cooley in
cooperation with the vulnerable Cooley, the Cooley who plays and the Cooley
who articulates an emotional and physical sorrow. "bodies are / tubers put
into darkness" (*Irene* 91). The persona grieves for his mother, notices the
world dissolving, millions of voices escaping. Her death kindles a musing on
transitory living, on "the few moments we have / to swing on our own bones."
Even while lamenting the briefness, he celebrates the bodily sensations that
come to us from inhabiting physical bodies. *Fielding* and *Irene*, which very
differently consider the lives and deaths of his father and mother, open up
the idea of the memoir to incorporate stories that deliver the very pages that
reproduce Orin and Irene. Cooley's questions lead to responses, and his
rejoinders tease and necessitate further provocative questions.

    Philosopher Karol Toeplitz disputes Descartes' notion "I think, therefore
I am" with his own maxim, "Respondeo ergo sum" (I answer, therefore I am).[9]
In an oral world, says Dennis Cooley, "a speaker speaks directly to an audience
and responds to that audience" (Bonar 3). Responding to his own writing, to
the poetry of others, to the expected replies/questions/comments by readers,
to the thought-provoking questions his poetics summon, Cooley's poetry is
already engaged, connected, absorbed in conversation. Toeplitz's idea that one
is continually in dialogue, shifts the Cartesian focus from decisive-mind to
one of social engagement. Dennis Cooley's poetry—from line to line, from
page to page, from book to book—gives the reader little choice. By turning
the pages, the reader abandons he/rself to the carnal pleasure of discourse, is
dragged in gleeful trepidation and sensual delight toward those "six impossi-
ble things before breakfast," is always "caught" in the middle of a conversa-
tion—with the poet or a neighbour or with the vampish poem. Cooley falls
and trips and tumbles eagerly over punctuation and prepositions and ono-
matopoeic delights. He lets readers mistake the terrain and rewrite the topo-
graphy of the body's fault lines, its leaky orifices, its visceral satisfactions.
Writes Cooley: "know that we are confirmed / in catastrophes of blood"

(*seeing red* 133), sustained by inherited catastrophes, through catastrophic tropes, within apostrophic blood ties. Cooley writes of spring as a "swollen moon" (*country music* 134), of *sunfall's* "blood lifting" ("Winnipeg in winter" 149) winter inhalation, and of blood clots whispering towards the vulnerable heart (*Irene* 45–46). He writes with the "muse of absence" and for readers' "a muse ment" (*Dedications* 79 and 80), he writes towards crooked veins and against "the lethal bubble" (*this only home* 90). Cooley composes and corresponds and as he creates he bleeds and clots and hemorrhages and beats and pulses. His words, hypodermic, seep through the poetic corpus. Cooley, the caught Burglar of the body's persuasive enjambments. His thefts scandalizing students and poetasters alike. Cooley, not just writing renegade, but converting into one. "What has been happening to poetry…?" Cooley asks. His answers incite more poetry, more play, more innovative language and lines and stanza breaks, and more poetic philandering. In *seeing red*, Cooley introduces the idea that a vampiric succubus drains the bourgeois of lifeblood ("a dismal scientist speaks" 81), revising the definition of birth and origins. In a poem named for the love of blood, poetry as a "barricade of blood" ("haemophilia" 117) traps breath, crosses the double-crosses, permeates words with oxygen, with the cinnamon moon, with gorgeous bones. Cooley's poems respond to each other, respond to me, compel me to respond, respond to the myriad of poetry that has come before and that pours out after. As each poem tantalizes with its responses, with more questions, Dennis Cooley nudges his readers to ponder, to write back, to reply. To *our* place. *Our* poems. Engorgeous.

—Nicole Markotić

Notes

1 I wish to thank Neil Besner, Brian Henderson, and Rosemary Nixon for our many conversations about Dennis Cooley's poetry and for their generous editing responses to this essay.

2 I begin, here, by speaking of the classroom to gesture towards Dennis Cooley's outstanding career as an English professor at the University of Manitoba, and as an opportunity to mention his enthusiasm, delight, and passion for teaching the poem, the page, the word.

3 In particular, Cooley's long poems (*Bloody Jack, Country Music, Fielding, Irene*) formalize the attention onto whose story gets told. Cooley has uniquely reshaped and redefined the role of prairie poetry within the nation that has become Canada; in fact, he has reshaped the very boundaries of what defines the limits of both nation and page.

4 Interestingly, identity based on "one drop of blood" has historically been an argument used both to restrict or preserve ideas of racial purity and to claim or withhold (tenuous) membership.

5 Says Davidson: "since Dracula's blood lust is gender blind, he is linked to homoerotic discourses, for which his effeminate and aristocratic qualities serve as markers" (46).

6 Published first in 1984, *Blood Jack* ended with a poem titled "Appendix." In the 2002 "reprint," newer, cheekier poems shuffle that final organ farther inside the body.

7 Cooley wrote on *The Collected Works of Billy the Kid* in *The Vernacular Muse*, and invokes Ondaatje's notion of the compelling bandit throughout many of the *Bloody Jack* poems.

8 Cooley-the-character chastises Jack for citing Kroetsch's *What the Crow Said*. Cooley appears troubled not only that Krafchenko believes birds talk, but also that he's managed to read a novel not yet published in 1913 (*"what the crow really said,"* 176).

9 I am grateful to religious studies scholar Vijaya Subramani, who pointed this article out to me in her master's thesis on *Rasa* theory.

Works Cited

Bernstein, Charles. "Optimism and Critical Excess (Process)." *A Poetics*. Cambridge: Harvard University Press, 1992. 150–178.

Bonar, Michael. "In Many Ways ... An Interview with Dennis Cooley." *Essays on Canadian Writing* 41 (Summer 1990):'1–15.

Bourdieu, Pierre. *The Rules of Art: Genesis and Structure of the Literary Field*. Translated by Susan Emanuel. Stanford: Stanford University Press, 1995.

Carroll, Lewis. *Through the Looking Glass: And What Alice Found There*. New York: Peter Pauper Press, 1940.

Cooley, Dennis. *the bentley poems*. Winnipeg: Pachyderm Press, 2000.

———. "Breaking and Entering (thoughts on line breaks)." *Open Letter* 6/7 (Spring 1987): 77–99.

———. *Burglar of Blood*. Winnipeg: Pachyderm Press, 1992.

———. *Bloody Jack*. Winnipeg: Turnstone Press, 1984.

———. *Bloody Jack*. Introduction by Douglas Barbour. Edmonton: University of Alberta Press, 2002.

———. Interview with Todd Bruce and Robert Budde. "Cooley Dreams His Way into the World: A Conversation." *Prairie Fire: Special Issue on Dennis Cooley*. Vol. 19, no. 1 (Spring 1998): 47–65.

———. *country music*. Vernon, BC: Kalamalka Press, 2004.

———. *Dedications*. Saskatoon: Thistledown Press, 1988.

———. *Fielding*. Saskatoon: Thistledown Press, 1983.

———. *goldfinger*. Winnipeg: Staccato, 1995.

———. *Irene*. Winnipeg: Turnstone Press, 2000.

———. *Leaving*. Winnipeg: Turnstone Press, 1980.

———. *passwords: transmigrations between canada and europe*. Kiel, Germany: 1&f Verlag, 1996.

———. *Perishable Light*. Regina: Coteau Books, 1988.

———. *seeing red*. Winnipeg: Turnstone Press, 2003.

———. *Soul Searching*. Red Deer: Red Deer College Press, 1987.

———. *sunfall*. Concord, ON: Anansi Press, 1996.

———. *this only home*. Winnipeg: Turnstone Press, 1992.

———. *The Vernacular Muse: the eye and ear in contemporary literature*. Winnipeg: Turnstone Press, 1987.

Davidson, Michael. "Strange Blood: Hemophobia and the Unexplored Boundaries of Queer Nation." *Beyond the Binary: Reconstructing Cultural Identity in a Multicultural Context*. Edited by Timothy Powell. New Brunswick, NJ: Rutgers University Press, 1999. 39–60.

Derrida, Jacques. "The Law of Genre." Translated by Avital Ronell. *Acts of Literature*. New York: Routledge, 1992. 221–253.

"The Gift." *Buffy the Vampire Slayer*. Written and Directed by Joss Whedon. 5th Season. DVD collection. Distributed by 20th Century Fox, 2005.

Kamboureli, Smaro. "Stealing the Text: George Bowering's 'Kerrisdale Elegies' and Dennis Cooley's 'Bloody Jack.'" *Canadian Literature* 115 (Winter 1987): 9–23.

Keahey, Deborah. *Making It Home: Place in Canadian Prairie Literature*. Winnipeg: University of Manitoba Press, 1998.

Kroetsch, Robert. "Don't Give Me No More of Your Lip; or, the Prairie Horizon as Allowed Mouth." *Toward Defining the Prairies: Region, Culture, and History*. Edited by Robert Wardhaugh. Winnipeg: University of Manitoba Press, 2001. 209–215.

Riding, Laura, and Robert Graves. *A Survey of Modernist Poetry*. London: Heinemann, 1927.

Toeplitz, Karol. "Respondeo Ergo Sum." *Dialogue and Universalism*. Vol. 7–8 (1997): 175–186.

Dennis Cooley Bibliography

Cooley, Dennis. *Andrew Suknaski; In the Name of Narid*. Editor. Erin: Porcupine's Quill, 1981.

———. *the bentleys*. Edmonton: University of Alberta Press, 2006.

———. *the bentley poems*. Winnipeg: Pachyderm Press, 2000.

———. *Burglar of Blood*. Winnipeg: Pachyderm Press, 1992.

———. *Bloody Jack*. Winnipeg: Turnstone Press, 1984.

———. *Bloody Jack*. Introduction by Douglas Barbour. Edmonton: University of Alberta Press, 2002.

———. *country music*. Vernon: Kalamalka Press, 2004.

———. *Dedications*. Saskatoon: Thistledown Press: 1988.

———. *Draft: An Anthology of Prairie Poetry*. Editor. Winnipeg: Turnstone Press, 1981.

———. *Eli Mandel and His Works*. Editor. Toronto: ECW Press, 1980.

———. *Fielding*. Saskatoon: Thistledown Press, 1983.

———. *goldfinger*. Winnipeg: Staccato, 1995.

———. *Inscriptions: A Prairie Poetry Anthology*. Editor. Winnipeg: Turnstone Press, 1981.

———. *Irene*. Winnipeg: Turnstone Press, 2000.

———. *Leaving*. Winnipeg: Turnstone Press, 1980.

———. *passwords: transmigrations between canada and europe*. Kiel, Germany: l&f Verlag, 1996.

———. *Perishable Light*. Regina: Coteau Books, 1988.

———. *RePlacing*. Editor. Toronto: ECW Press, 1980.

———. *seeing red*. Winnipeg: Turnstone Press, 2003.

———. *Soul Searching*. Red Deer: Red Deer College Press, 1987.

———. *sunfall*. Concord, ON: Anansi Press, 1996.

———. *this only home*. Winnipeg: Turnstone Press, 1992.

———. *The Vernacular Muse: the eye and ear in contemporary literature*. Winnipeg: Turnstone Press, 1987.

A Poem for You, Leaving Winnipeg

for three slim summers
      you wore
the burn of land
    blown lean
    by the wind's bend
      filled with
        the sun's bare circle
    that pulled the darkness
    from your bloodslow cycle.

      was it fire
        for you
    (from your
      English air and rain)
        turning the long
        bright winters of snow and ice
      late summers of green/brown heat
          hard and fast
        here among us.

now you are leaving
    in the hanging fullness of
      our August life
        (palegreen sprouts   skinred roots
          thicken and bulge sweet with
        juices sucked from earth and sky)
   and you ask for
  some words to wear
      more than the easy talk
        you have always heard
    hurt that you found
      in me (raised
        in this prairie light) nothing

```
           to show  /  to spare
       a poem for you
     nothing to take
                 with you wanting
                       to know and
                            be known.
```

anaeurysm

a permanent abnormal blood-filled dilation

of a blood vessel resulting from disease of

the vessel wall

    & we are skinbags of heated water   dreaming

                brains grayly

        balloon in our heads

                  nerves skein   blind

                  albino seaweed blown

          in our bodies' pools

                    listening

          carbon phases / your phrases

              strung between us father

        your breath tumbles

              shining quiet

       inside my ribs

    find your hand hard in mine

        your lines wound in

              the stretch of my muscles

      still living

in his tangerine skin

we buried him
in mint condition
on his eyes
two georges
they shone like hens eyes
he inhaled the dark
hhhhgg hhggg
engorged it
like a badger breathing
for blood
when we shovelled him in
christ he was a gorgeous man
the eyes were breathing
& shining blood

the love song of j l krafchenko or the trans canada in (trance crypt

crossing

hhhoo   yyyooooooooooo   hhoo   yyYoooOOooOOOO

poosh ka   poosh ka   poosh

_____

_____

po o sh ka   po os hk a

HOO

train at the level

coupling

pooshka   pooShka   pOoshKA   PoSHkA   POSHkA

_____

_____

end for end

poo sh ka   Poo SH kA   POO SH K A   POOSH KA

YOOOOOOOOOOOOO   OOOOOOO

Sonya Orlowsky

They say in Plum Coulee there's this old Ukrainian lady she
can cure cancer. You know the Mennonites how they are always
comin down with some kind of sickness or other. One time it's
pneumonia, nother time it's they're simple in the head. Not
one thing it's another. That's why they keep lookin for other
men, the women there. Somethin about needin new blood on
account of they're always marrying each other that causes all
kinds of troubles for them—so babies dead when they're born
or they've got one leg shorter than the other maybe or they've
got their eyes crossed, that sort of thing. Sure, some people say
they go just crazy at times the women there sometimes they're
kind of mixed up crabby with women's troubles I guess and
wantin dark men somethin bad but I dunno, can't say about
that one.

Anways, this lady, Sonya Orlowsky's her name, she's Ukrainian
and she can cure cancer, that's what they say at least. You
might know her, remember she was just, well, one good-lookin
woman at one time, apparently, they say, back round the 80's
the one you musta heard it when Garry Reed left his wife and
six kids and ran off with that dark woman well that was her,
caused a real stink with his folks, never talked to him after,
not once in all those years since then. Funny, n she the best
liked schoolteacher district ever had too. Still got a way with
men, I mean that's the story you get at any rate, isn't it?

But that's not what I was gonna tell ya. She has this, I dunno,
this watchemecallem, a kind of power I guess you'd say. Ever
since she was 13, 14 and startin to turn a few heads in town
she's had it. It's kind of strange I mean a guy doesn't know what
to make of it eh but, well, they say she just puts her hand on
the growth, real gentle, always right hand for some reason
I hear. Say it's on the neck here and she'll just hold it there for

awhile, maybe 2, 3 minutes say and then, when she lifts it, the
growth 's gone. It's in her hand there, just like a small white octopus
they say. But the crazy thing is there's not sposed to be any scar left
over. It's gone, every last sign of it's completely gone. Hands like
that. I know that's hard to believe but I've talked to dozens of
people from out that way and they all say that's what happens,
they swear to God it's true, every last one of them swears that she
just lifts the hand and there it is the cancer's gone, just like that.
Layin right there in her hand.

Think that's amazin, wanna hear something really strange? All
the people, all the ones had those growths removed, know what
they do after? They go and pickle them. That's right, they put
them up in jars and set them in their sitting room where
everyone can see them. Callin by Karl Dyck's and his missus
the other day, day it rained, week ago Tuesday must a bin,
to pick up some eggs and there she was—a big white blob in
this sealer, right there plop on top of the radio. Karl was pretty
pleased about it, took down the jar and give it to me so's I
could get a good look at it floatin round like a pig's foot in
vinegar. Don know what he was thinkin but did he get a kick
out of it, but to tell the truth it give me the willies. Got no
stomach for them things but I guess it don bother the Dycks one
little bit, they just passed it round like was one of those big
French parsnips if you ever seen one of them, seemed to think
it was somethin special we were all sposed to drop our drawers
at or somethin. Funny thing 's even the little girl, what's her
name, the little one always giggles, yeah—Caroline, Caroline
she watched it like she was a cat fishin, know how they just
sit there and stare and stare.

Paul sd   .

souls were sneezes
that snooze in dough of bodies

waitful as helium and dream
of release in lesions and wild
explosions of membranes
that tuck them (fearful babies) in

a lot of souls were snuff
snorted up by stained & smelly bodies
where they snored their lives away

souls (generally) were badgers that sat bad
tempered in the tunnels of your body

mute as nutmeg
some of them snuggled in
faces full of chutney and blood pudding

gentler souls were gophers
waiting for easter to spring them
free & easy as   electric pogo sticks

& sinners were
everywhere sinners were
out of breath
with riotous living

they slept in bodies
like CO_2 cartridges

thats what sinners were

Exorcism

i am poured out like water
and my bones are unbuckled
my throat is dried up
bricks when you hold them

the crouch of dogs they circle
me they dig into
my hands and feet
i can count all my bones
they finger my bones
and at the sight they open their mouths
at me nothing hidden from whose blue eyes
and whose mouth comes fire forth

give back lustre to mine
eyes lest i sleep
in death for all
that lean against me
thou hast smitten
on the cheek thou hast
the teeth of sinners
smashed their breath

need only bestir and then
they are scattered
as smoke is driven
away so do they
vanish as wax
is melted so do they
like snows of flax
shatter in thy breath
by fire in their tents
of skin
      the hissing out

in fall the fields of flax
from the mouth of night
    spun over
           night into gold

   & the sky & the wind
      & the spirits spurt

I think "ego"; ergo I am

                              I think so
                              I think
                                it is
                              so
                                i think
          let us begin
          by considering the most
          common things the bodies
          we touch and see

          let us take this piece
          of wax from the hive

          it has not yet lost
          the sweetness of honey
          it still retains something
          the smell of clover

          it is hard cold it is
          tangible and if one breaks
          it or taps
          it it will emit
          a certain sound so
          all things
          can be known

                    but as I am
                    speaking it is
                    placed near a flame
                    what remains of its taste
                    peels off easy
                    as a banana skin lets go
                    the fragrant smell crashes
                    away its pale yellow

scrapes its shape loose grows
bigger becomes
        (soft with meaning)
liquid warms up you
can hardly touch
it and if furred
with fire i tap it again
and again it will
no longer make a
        any sound

        except when i put it
        to my ear i hear
        the sound of sun   roaring
        like a marigold

labiarinth

travelling west

thru alberta this was
you could tell
everyone looked
funny everywhere you looked

hay   look Megan said
& we looked & saw
the road the road you could
see   the way was paved
way to hell & gone it was
        /paved

does Kroetsch know this
I said well actually I didnt
say this as a matter of fact I thot
about that road for a long
long time it damn near
drove me crazy

the road that long
long road was paved
every goddamn inch
                    of it

thru Alta this was
you could tell

the way was paved

anatomy of love
for michael

when his brain
  michael would say
crashes or his heart
  vehicles blood
it is the centrifuge of love

love motors the magneto brain
   ticking ticking
 roars and clashes
one of those muscle cars at a stop
      light waiting
  the aorta bright and red
as a police cruiser
   which pulls you over for speeding

on top at the end
  a little bruise of blood its
    radiant
 bruise of love

      is pulsing
  && thuds the others
 where their faces stand around
   watchful as horses

prairie romance

                                        dawn comes
                        on rubber tires
        in bull low
                        a grain truck growling
            up the sky
                            shifts
                into second   begins to trot
                            at coffee break   down the lane
                into third glides at a canter
        the roaddust where we eat
                            sardine & onion sandwiches
                    the jig of day

            soon its sun
        galloping across the 1:30 news

                & lather gathers
        & the horse in overdrive is loose under the hood
                        & running & running under the sun
                the chaff of sun
                            drives us to elevators
            & drying   fielddust   our skin   & our sweat where we
        ride
            & ride the shimmer of gas & horseflesh

                    & at night
                        the light
            drops out
                a wrecked transmission
                    spilling oil

                    & we are left
                country kids (horse
            power to burn

                                spinning
                        & spinning

                the pavement of night

behind the door

                bodies preferred to think of themselves
                crowding cheek by jowl
            into barns jewelled with grain
            heavy   hay & a farmer to keep them
            warm & fed to bring them newly
            born into   rooms of horn & hoof
                rut and root rain on the roof
                            of their brains

        "to keep seed alive upon the face of all the earth"

        animals
                    girdled in the cluck
            & moon of milk
                        egg white of cat & pigeon
                            eyeblink & heartslump
                                    animals were muscles
                        made throatnoises through the lump
                                            of months
        secret in the stomach of wood

                they arced or folded
                    in ecstacy   eyes
            flooded with oil
        when the farmer touched them
                    nuzzled their chins & udders
                                    in winter
                        inside ribs of wood
                            pails of water

                spoke to them
                language of grass & sun
        what in the nights that are long
                husbands to   wives say

                     of grass & sun
              & the opening of gates
                          of summer   in them
the way water sits   when it is almost ice

animals were leather
                       the farmer wore
          close to his heart

                          they were
         pouches   filled with tobacco
                              in his dream
     vests he wore   to church

          at night they spoke   silently
         to one another
    the bodies dangled like babies
                     in the hump of barn

standing & standing in puddles of time

              weight of nights   wet
                    as sand

& when January punched at them
              sandbagged snow against their eyes
                     they lay down   into the sweet
        grunt of straw that melodied   dreams
hidden   in   hides

              the paunch of dark
                   the lazy   lift of time
        left like smoke   in the   crease   of dreams

                     all that long waiting

        bodies were blood in a barn of bone

moon musings

                              moons
: a grape on wedgewood
: frozen lettuce
: a thumb print on carbon paper
: a glass of gin in an all star cast
: a pimple   on ms. cynthia harpers bum
: a meringue pie
: a turtle plopped on mud
: a moth   chewing on my blankets
: a cashew   before its eaten
: a flashlight in gods fist making his rounds for the night

: a tap spraying frost over our heads
: a blimp of dough
: a bagel from elis deli
: an alka seltzer tablet fizzing
: a butter tart   full of raisins   for whatever reasons
: a clam   cracked open)this is a pearl that was(
: a battery post powdered with acid
: a wad of double bubble gum
: a nickel melting with cold
: an Amazons breast

: an Amazons nipple playing me for a sucker & me just trying
   to keep abreast of current affairs
: a wholewheat muffin   & good for you
: a western buckle on gods britches   a button too
: a slop pail of piss and ashes
: a clicker on gods heel   you like his moves
: a hole acetylened in steel
: a leprous forehead
: a sugar cookie half eaten by bumsteads daughter
: an aspirin
: a chickens eye watching us the head chopped off & peeking thru

: a lid off a campbells soup tin
: a tumour in gods brain
: a wornout balloon   its skin sloppy
: a used bladder
: a fingernail pared off of gods forefinger
: a scab picking it off his foot
: a vacuum hose sucking dandruff & skin sloughings
  off the earth
: a one-way disk badly rusted in the field
: a sheeps eyeball seen from the back where the fat
  & veins are
: a wastebasket earth puts its garbage in

: a gland secreting secret juices & brain waves
: a netted gem potato
: a carbuncle on gods neck
: a car rattling thru the night a model T one headlight
  burned out & the sky shaking under it
: a hub cap hubba hubba ding ding
: an eye staring thru the curtain
: a dead mouth on a microphone & he cant hear you/
  hes not listening
: a wrinkle of pus in chicken skin
: a belly button where earth broke away from the sky
: a sack of knobbled fat   Laws of the Starry Heavens

: a jelly bean chewing
: a snuff box
: pineal pinned in the brain of god   a frog splayed on the sky
: a sucker wedged   nudging in mud
: flops in a flap pita bread a pocket of light
: a phosphorescent watch on gods wrist
: a gurgle gargle in his mouth
: a wart on an angels neck
: a tear on the face of night
: a vowel from some tuba or saxophone blown
: got her eye on me
: a kid with soap bubbles

: frisbee on fast film rivetted on the plate of night
: an eye in the head of a lizard
: cabbage frozen in the fridge
: the sardonic/skeptical eye of a hen thats lost its head
: an almond snapped out of its skin
: a pill of cod liver oil
: a capsule/ampule of bath oil
: a red cross sac of blood

: an analgesic dropped in coke
: a piece of american chicken   yellow with fat
: a spot in a liver
: knocked up   with light
: pickerel cheek (of local reference)
: a spot where a horse stepped off in mud & its frozen
: a hunk of hail   a jag of ice
: a block fallen off the icemans wagon & he shld be on/   the wagon
: a scab where air has skinned its knees
: the foot of a persian cat

: a shopping bag woman   sagging with starch
: a gunny sack   full of spuds
: a potato (boiled)
: a burr snagged on a priests robe
: a cup of milk gone sour
: the sacred face of a child scarred in the dark mouth agape
: a cancerous lung
: a balloon face   floating
: a belly button to other spheres
: a fanny a fat ladys fanny flashed in an inner tube (swimming)
: a vertebra/knuckle of light
: a bug stuck in oil
: a pumpkin grinning pork-faced
: a pouch of tobacco / a tobacco pouch
: a taco   full of cheese
: a salt lick
: a beached whale

: a pan of milk   black cat lapping
: an earlobe   packed with fat & hyperbole
: a balloon a child moves pulling it after

: a magic stone gazes through wallets of space
: an eye of a cat open in sleep/death
: an astrolabe taking its bearings on earth
: a sugared apricot
: a ball bearing earth turns on at night
: lube in a tube
: a pigs snout   hairy with loveliness
: snot on carbon paper
: in heat secretes its lotions goes thru the motions
: lube in a tube

: an onion mired in mud
: a 53 Merc one headlight shot on the backroads of Moose Jaw
: opens a hole with the aplomb of a searchlight: a flash light
   plummets & plumbs the basement & lovers skitter crazy as silver
   fish on skates for cover
: the dial of a telephone you cld call god
: a hubcap (hubbahubba) rattling where its spun off on blacktop
   ding ding
: glad tidings to all

holy cow

```
                  hey   rune
            diddle               the
           fiddle                 for
            the                   straight
            rat                   went
            and                   wish
            the                   the
          riddle                  and
            the                   dark
            now                   such
         jumped                   see
           over                   to
             the                  laughed
              moon             bat
                  the    little
```

inner ear

    once you have been
           there
    all the blood

    your head brooded
        as nightbirds
        with blood
          your life floats
            in arrears

          & you have seen
sun   moon   stars
    the earth

          you come back
             almost afraid
  to touch
          any thing

    wanting more than
        anything
      to touch

              your ear a shoe
             full of blood

my eye

that's you out there (all eyes)
fly on the sky we can see you
you little grunt there
where you sigh and bleep
you babble your bibless sleep
burp your way across the roof
through night air we long to have
you back & to let you go forever
bleating heart beating beating
at the door lemme in lemme in

what do you see child
you and your wide eyes
will you turn on your parents
turn your parents in
to charcoal in black and white
we should put you up
for adoption you

small gust in the night
chill in our dreams
lethal bubble in the blood

melodious rhyme

                                   fair enough
                                        if you
insist
                      this

rhyming Melodie
                                  yes it
is
                      there
                                  for the
reading
            it is here   the writing
too

if you are ready
                                      && if not

                             not
what can i say what would you have me
say it is a crime the way things fall

                vein vain venal venus
                raven ravenous venous

                                  take that
        then
                yes the sweet red
                river sweet as straw
                berry we build cities beside
                marry the unmanageable blood

                      all the blood
                  the whole story
               the whole bloody thing

all of it, singing

                the woods ringing

                                                    −minstrel

menstrual

        so to   construe
there at the tip   our tongues
here at the top   of our lungs
    the ministering   words
     time & time   again
    the murdering   rhymes
      you lap up   love
     to run   your tongue
       over   & over

he replies to his critics

why does it so offend you
i should say the moon
is a gland, perhaps mammary,
that it secretes over us
something we cannot see

is a poultice and draws
out of us strange secretions
moves us to strange feelings

what do you want from me
that the moon should be
a clear drop of amber
a bone china plate
that tings, elegantly, when you
ding it a dinner bell a wine decanter
is this what you want
all you can tolerate

is it that unthinkable
i should say of her face
it is rough it is tubercular

why does this upset you
why though you protest
do you lash why
do you think
i should not say this
why do you allow so little

all the cosmetics you would
paste over the cosmos

breathless

       though you do not know
       you wear me on your neck
       think you can keep me off
                safe as a cuff
       link & as presentable

       all along you are stringing
                me along there
                the chain of garlic
                close to your heart

       why is this why am i
       always crossed in love

                am a muzzle of time
                        i know

       i make quite an impression
                i know that
                there's no denying
                the way i hit you
                        sudden
                get a word in
                blood clot you can feel
       me beating
                breathing
       deep in your heart

In Germany cooley is a migrant labourer. His small brain.

Remember, months later, back in Winnipeg, Dana has told me this before—kuli is pen—and it dropped out of my brain like a chair knocked over. And that Heidi of the haircut taught me my first German sentence, said good you said it just like a german. Der Stuhl. Cooley was sitting on der stuhl, he said he needed to, go to stuhl. Sshh she said. Sit very Stuhl.

> Cooley's brain penned up
> pensive pens ive
> used mused with pen
> ultimately he is getting used
>   to it in
> ti mately he will
> have been is am
> used only later much
> later does he think
> he has set it up
> again

Wished we had the camera for David. Many other paintings we're
happy to see.

                    just out
                  & the feeling
                    you have
                   your body

              falling out from under
              a sling or a hammock &
              it could be strung through
                    your spine
                  the way it feels

                        the ends get un
                      done it cld be un
                          der wear &
                      it all falls down

        a pillow case you have
     slept weeks on & you are left
        holding the pillow or a
            tired angel on
          her feet for hours
            without break
            her beak too
            tired to sing

    After, wandering around the Marienplatz, cool day, on the
verge of rain, there are spots of rain, people gathering to see the
intricate clockworks high on the city hall go off, street entertainers,
one an American voice throwing hoops higher & higher into the air.
    Before that we see a dancer in the park turning & turning &
turning inside the gazebo the cool air light rain falling.

winnipeg in winter

iron lungs in the basement
blood lifting

every room
breathing through teeth

lines rooms like wallpaper
climbs the stairs

cold in its mouth tumbles down

under the cold sky
winter a giant & sleeping body
fitted with stars
we move slowly all winter in

moonlight sour as cider

though we are patient, wait the season
sounds it makes, alive
thoughts move in & out
pass through skin & bones
relieved to be out
to be in
the skin we curtain our lives with

moves inside
our lives
/ short of air
the way we inhale
the way we inhale
one another
the way we are made
\ whole
almost
mad   we are
that close

a series of shocking pre-positions
& after

                              words

            to place be
                              fore
                                                    or in
                              front
            of:

            about   be low   from   to
            above   beneath   in   to ward
            after   beside   in side   through
            ahead   betwixt   off   through out
            around   between   on   under
            at   by   out   until
            a way   down   over   up
            back   during   past   with
            before   for   since   within
                        behind

had we but word enuff:

                    to   before   in   of
                         place   or   front

                                                      & time

                         time &
            time again
                                        this
                                        my lady
                    would be

mother tongue
        we learn
              to speak
     yearn to talk

at our mother's breast
we learn to say something
you coax us into

    take our first
shaky
        steps
into talk

walk on air
      again
  & again
       try to speak
         our mother
     tongue tied
        so to speak
   inside this room
     tied to you
  we try &
      nurse you
  back to breath

can hardly
    talk
hardly say
  a thing
dare not
  breathe
a word

this on remembrance weekend:

there is a blood clot
in the tunnel it flutters
hovers there /red scarf
blood gusts & breezes

they hope to melt with poison
they now call perfume
the red silk rustling inside you
whispers of romance
that would kill

it could be a cloud on a fence
it could be net stockings

fear if it breaks
it will go straight
to your heart
slip through

silk stocking in wind
innocent as a nightcap
catching the direction
stop all flight

that it will blow up
against the lung
when it hits
the way to breath
will take your breath away

only we know it doesn't
know the way to your heart
has no way of knowing you
are a woman of few vanities
it has no way of reaching
any corner of your longing
never to wear the red silk
where it flutters

a dying bird
just below your throat

bodies are
tubers put into darkness
darkness blots up time
you cannot peel off like tape

darkness could be a worker
taking up old carpets
POP **POP** POP POP
flesh unsnapped from bones

voices dissolve in soil
wash away in rain words as if they never were
spoken before as they never will again
not though we call till we can speak no more

all we know is
time for a time hangs

the sweet flesh   hums
bright fish   feeding at coral

and then
millions & millions of voices
run away
go back to the sea back to the waters back into sun
a moment exhaled on breath
all the voices flesh & bone have made

nothing we can say
can rinse the darkness off
talk flesh back into time
the yard calling
rooms crying out
children talking
taking their time
the few moments we have
to swing on our bones

jack's dictionary of cunning linguists

novitiate: a johnny come lately
rabid: foaming at the mouth
aging: can't afford to lose face / agen
despondent: is sunk in depression
effete: a poet taster, nosegay some would have it
swinging: lets down his hair
puritanical: her lips are sealed
conscientious: gives 'm a fair shake
tonsorial: gets in the hair
impetuous: dives in head-first
indifferent: gives the cold shoulder
radical: in a hot bed of activity
reckless: headed for a crackup
hard-up: has trouble making ends meet
bilingual: is beside herself, he speaks with a forked tongue
turbulent: is often feeling floosie
disapproving: favours a crackdown
outstanding: is head and shoulders above
myopic: can't see beyond his nose
meek: turns the other cheek
loyal: sticks it out through thick & thin
bankrupt: goes belly up
clumsy: hits it right on the nose
marginal: involved in split decisions
timid: won't find fault with anyone
hermaphroditic: really comes into herhishisher own
inquisitive: an eager beaver
thorough: doesn't want to leave anything out
lesbian: speaks in the mother tongue
sentimental: lives in nether nether land
optimistic: believes s/he is making head way
sadistic: always beats it
moralistic: makes snap judgements

reformed: gets a weight off herhis shoulders
journalistic: gives a blow by blow account
inexperienced: fuzzy faced
parsimonious: speaks with pursed lips the tightwad
truculent: holds herhis own
proletarian / fallen / cursed: lives by the sweat of his brow
divine: she brings down the world on his head
experienced: fuzzy faced
fed up: will tell him/her where to get off
tempted: within an inch of his wife
angry: cuts off his nose to spite his face
lucky: experiences a windfall
promiscuous: has a loose tongue
                    likes a loose tongue too
malcontented: airs grievances
impatient: plays hard and fast
hypocritical: is two-faced
epicurean: develops a taste for it
enterprising: 'd snap you up in a minute, a split second
inventive: eager to find a new wrinkle, vents her views
witty: a real wag with women
speculative: gets caught in boom & bust
aboriginal: is leary of pale faces
investigative: an undercover agent
                    fears someone will blow her cover
sadomasochistic: deals is dealt a heavy blow
                    catches you in one hell of a tongue-twister
acrobatic: goes into a nose dive
                    a tail spin
English: keeps a stiff upper lip
equivocal: faces a split decision
aggressive: knows you can never get off easy
duplicitous: between a lick and a promise
Freudian: trusts in a slip of the tongue
harried: sometimes s/he's all in
competitive: busy nosing out rivals
snotty: looks down his nose at

narcissistic: the spitting image
lucky: wins by a nose
despondent: down in the mouth
correspondent: keeps in touch
premature: finds things are touch and go
impatient: always beats it
traditional: is above that sort of thing
reserved: makes no bones about it
        will tell him/her where to get off
athletic: calling audibles in the huddle (jocular asides)
       sure sure I have a glib & fluid tongue so do you you
       too for my part I am voluble [fr. *volvere* to roll;
       akin to oe wealwian to roll, Gk *eilyein* to roll, wrap]
       hence a rolling tongue & yr rollin over wrapt as in
       vulva [integument, womb; akin to Skt ulva womb, L
       vol-vere to roll—more at VOLUBLE] to speak up, to pipe
       up a pipe dream, blowing bubbles & she is forever
       blowing me, to roll yr r's my bonnie lass; to babble on
religious: wholly committed
devout: holy thine
macho: hard nosed
offensive: rubs people the wrong way
rude: can't keep a civil tongue in his head
humbled: faces a real come down
improvident: up to the chin in
fickle: blows hot and cold
casual: comes breezing in at the last moment
uncoordinated: way out of whack
disadvantaged: is really up against it
unskilled: a fringe player
venturesome: lets down the hair
over bearing: baring down on him
rabid: foaming at the mouth fomenting trouble
confused: doesn't know what's eating her
fierce: she'd box his ears
legalistic: issues sub poenas

opportunistic: johnny on the spot
                    blows his chances
athletic: breezes thru the warm ups / the preliminaries
exploitive: plays you for a sucker
Catholic: gets into bad habits
jocular: does laps to stay in shape
                lip/lap lip/lap lip/lap
French: wins by default

        :

vain:

        ::

    : really lays one on you

    : two faced

disloyal: does an about face

    : lays it on a little thick
    : sticks with you through thick & thin

    I M : U :: U R : B

blood brothers

yes I was there I always am
there when he tears
throats & the ditch fills

the creak of wings
crows coming to watch

we bend & sip the voices
dampen our thoughts
we are glad after all
it is a time to talk

relieved to find our voices
have been hiding
all along beside us

the blood in throats
whizzes past like ghosts

a wetting of lips
a thickness of throats
an incessant speaking
in tongues

red men ace

      yeah well what do you expect
    him & cooley they're in cahoots

    i mean open yr eyes fer chrissake
bloody reds course they stick together

        they want ya tuh believe
they are harmless they got bad press
        Dracula he's just a poor
        misunderstood little boy

          don't you believe it
    they're bloody well dangerous
           contagious is what

   they know damn well what they're up to
      you ask me, wanna stuff their faces
        & don't lift a finger to earn it
          want a piece of yr pro
            perty is what
            in perpetuity
            can't wait to lay
                  a hand on it

      got to hand it to them on a platter
     it's public enterprise and nothing but

  want it so bad they can taste it
     them & them bleedin'
       heart liberals

echolalia

                              the first thing you should know
                              about me is   i am
                              a sound poet
                                        i wind up &
                              throw my voice
                    into the tent
              : like that

    ? how you like that
                    neat don't you think
          all the loops in the system

        some smart guy said well
    what's the point
              it's canvas isn't it
            & you say yeah well so what
              it's paint yr smearing there
          all over the canvas yr words are paint

    he's a real pain in the ass that guy

                    the important thing is
                        i take soundings see
                    i try to hear myself
                        try to hear you hearing
              yur eyes grow green & big
                that's how i find myself that's how
                        i find you
                  i can hear where you sizzle
            & pop

the red
emption of blood

                    sure i am
                  they're right
                      i am
                a burglar of blood
        bugler of salivation the seventh seal busted
                 there can be no X
                    emption
           before the distant & indistinct roar

       come as doctor, would relieve the pressure
       a little loyal bleeding, it's good for the realm

           you should spend some time on me
         to redeem currency it is a holy thing I do
           these transactions withdrawals from
           the banks the sepulchres your bodies
                    have become

         would take things into my own hands
               break open what is
             within you to give , tithing

            broadcast in a barren land
            bright coins of your blood

&
not that he's wrong
he's got a point
to tell the truth
i myself have been scheming
dream of never returning
from recess running out
way to heck and gone past the railway
junction reckless as a runaway hen
headed straight for the river
smell of baloney & butter
on my hands skipping
my knees skinned &
dipping for snakes
skinny dipping with all
the young rakes
all the way to zanzibar all of the aches going
and coming and
allen and andy and alex
i have laid
eyes on them
and would it had been hands
they were such handsome fellows

but most of all
oh most of all
randy and he
me and randy
smooth as cornsilk
and who'd believe me he
slippery as houdini
up & asked me

wouldi wouldi wouldi wouldi wouldi wouldi wouldi wouldi wouldi

whispered in my ear all the way
to vernon train
jerking under us
past trees snow had
fallen into sweetness of
their breath past
the hard darkred cherries
hung in bunches by peaches
lanterns someone had hung in the branches
all along the hills
apricots with their soft fuzzy skin
all the way barebummed into kalamalka lake
in plain sight of the mackie place
goose-bumped with the water up to my nipples
hard in the air him too saying yes
yesyes yesyes yesyesyesyes yesyes oh
my god yesyes yesyes yesyes

&
a crate of apples could i suppose
do it
create fall and before that spring
air of prairie in may
mayhem when red swallows
slip the sky knead it
into their houses
their thoughts of mud & straw & somewhere apples
white as snow already on the trees
dangle from their green syllabaries
chapters of worms & stars

what happens is
crow bars the way
crow spots a small crack in night
the lid dark and sealed with lacquer
pries his way in
beak & all
prayerful as his black robes allow
digs in &
heaves

breaks open the box light is nailed in

and it begins

a thin strip of veneer
on the horizon
by july it is burnt sugar

&

listening to night sticky with sweat the brown head glows
with what it has said and heard the air in which moths thud
on screens light becomes yellow & hissy says uh huh talks
talks through the fabric curtain it's hidden behind speaks
in voices that sound certain listens in on flights of static all
the pops and groans grow ecstatic and there are buzzes and
rowlings and they make what you might call a terrible racket
could be cats come from outer space the other side of the
moon or birds they're that far off and all trying to speak at
once so eager they talk over one another take over the room
speckle it with their voices that spot by spot form a shell we
talk inside a thin elastic the light in their voices warping

after words

Reader:

    I suppose we could start by asking you: where did you start as a poet?

Writer:

    Well I don't really know.

Reader:

    Your early experiences of being a poet, I mean. Was there maybe a teacher or a parent who got you on to poetry?

Writer:

    OK. My mom and dad read a lot, my dad especially. He had only taken grade 6 and had to leave school because his parents wanted him on the farm. Or didn't believe in education, I don't know which. I remember one time just before he died, about the only time he talked about it, he didn't say much, he never did, but I could hear hurt in his voice, and anger. Anyway he was a reader and he read mostly westerns and science fiction, but he read different stuff too. He'd be in from the field for dinner and he'd sneak in a little reading after he'd eaten, get so engrossed he was pretty much unaware of anything else. My mom, who had taken grade 11, which was pretty advanced for someone at that time in a poor farming and mining town, never read as much, probably because she got almost no time for her own. (Later, she read a lot, and took great pleasure in word games.) I also had a fabulous teacher for grades 4 to 8. Mr. Third. He believed with a passion in reading and writing and he had an enormous lot to do with what happened to me. One of the best times for all of us in that schoolroom—and we were a varied and straggly lot let me tell you—was when after noon hour he would read to us. We groaned when he stopped, wished he would never stop reading.

Reader:

    I wonder if you could say a bit more about where those interests took you and how they brought you into poetry?

Writer:

    Slowly, indirectly. By sheer chance quite likely. My dad said to me one day: what are you going to be when you grow up? I must have been 9 or 10 then, and by this time, doing well at school. (The first three grades were shaky for me, I think. I found school strange and bewildering at first.) I hadn't given it much thought really, but I remember saying mechanic, mechanic or truck driver. They seemed to me something special. No you're not, says my dad, you're going to university. I had no idea what that was but right then and there I knew I was going to university. When I got to high school I didn't do much reading and I did no writing whatsoever, no poetry that is, and very little of any kind. I was busy with jobs and sports and eventually romance, and helping my dad at the school where he had become janitor when we moved into town in 1958, part of the drastic wipe-out of the family farm in rural Saskatchewan. But I did know I was going to university, and later I knew I was going to be a teacher and I was going to specialize in English and biology, biology probably because my sister, Lynn, was at the U of Saskatchewan studying biology (and mathematics).

Reader:

Could you tell us more about school, what it was for you?

Writer:

I always loved learning poems by heart in public school, read with pleasure the ones in our readers and with a special sense of finding the Canadian poems which had not yet been obliterated from school books. And at university I loved English classes, saw my first honest-to-goodness writer, Earle Birney, met a couple of people who were actually writing. One thing led to another and through a series of accidents I ended up taking an honours degree and then a master's at Saskatchewan and finally a PhD at Rochester in New York state, where in 1971 I wrote a dissertation on the American poet Robert Duncan.

A few years later I arrived at the University of Manitoba and that's where things really broke open for me. I was teaching poetry, loving it. I was also writing about it, and I got caught up in the wild whirl of Canadian literature at Manitoba in the 1970s. Those were exuberant ebullient years when everything could happen, we could do everything we thought, and the rambunctious bunch at St. John's College came close to doing everything. Classes in Canadian writing were exploding in number and enrollment. Canadian writers were coming through, in one year a new writer each week, and that was heady and exhilarating. So were the writers-in-residence we had in those days. Dorothy Livesay, as writer-in-residence, member of faculty, goad, mentor, editor of cvii, was crucial to those early days. I became involved in the beginnings of a new press, Turnstone, for which I edited a batch of titles. I wrote a few reviews for new magazines in town, cvii and *Arts Manitoba*.

You can see where this is going. This vortex of energy and possibility was there, especially among a gang of young academics and graduate students in Canadian literature, and it released me into poetry: hey, maybe I can do this too? Reading those manuscripts was enabling, I think, as were my friends, above all David Arnason, a colourful and dynamic man who believed in Canadian writing and who immediately befriended me. Robert Kroetsch arrived with his intelligence and daring and passion, and his reputation did a lot to protect us. The occasion couldn't have been more propitious—all that activity, all that purpose and passion. It was a magical decade, the seventies, and I started writing.

The first title, *Leaving*, came out in 1980 as a chapbook. I was really late getting going, I was 38 then, and I was very uncertain about how it would be received, the chapbook I mean, and very nervous when I first read from it.

Reader:

    But why did you begin to do the things you do? Your poems strike me as a bit of an adventure for the reader.

Writer:

    I guess they are a bit odd, aren't they? I know at least one writer who is embarrassed to the point of offence, and more than a few readers who claim they can't get into them.

Reader:

    So, can you explain why this is the case? What is it that you are doing that creates these effects? Is it a matter of style? Tone? Voice?

Writer:

    I don't quite know why some readers balk. I guess the typography might have something to do with it. Topography too. Though I've had such little luck getting publishers to observe my fonts that there hasn't been a lot of that in what has gotten into print. A lot has to do with expectations, probably. If the poems look odd on the page—jagged margins, a scatter of letters— I can see where at first they might draw back. That and the light punctuation and unorthodox spelling. But other writers do this too and no one recoils from what they are doing. cummings took a run at these things a long time ago now. And the French even earlier.

Reader:

    Would it be fair to say that you write so many kinds of poems that there is no typical Cooley style?

Writer:

Yeah, I do all sorts of things, including stuff that most poets who think of themselves as formally adventurous, would bridle at. I love the lyric, a form we're told time and again is dead. I even write the odd song or rhymed and metred piece. Mostly I'd say I work with open form that ranges from the exuberantly oral and bawdy to the hesitant and inward. I believe in taking chances, pushing the poem. A lot of the poems are metalingual, many of them respond to something in the prairies. Many of them are begotten by other texts, or written as parts of longer poems. Inasmuch as my work has been characterized by mildly attentive readers, it has been thought of as vernacular and comical I'd imagine. If so, I may be partly responsible for that notion. I've written in defence of vernacular as a basis for poetry, and when I read I tend to choose the narrative and playful pieces.

Reader:

Why is that? Why do you do that—read those funny ones?

Writer:

Listeners can readily connect with them. That plus my own pleasure in reading them. I love those voices, I really do, and I think they can be fresh and full of energy. I take crazy joy in the mad spillage of sounds and I guess there is something compulsive in all that play. But I steer clear of other ones also because I find them emotional (and I often do, when they're very close to me: my family, friends. *Irene* and *Fielding* would be examples). I soon get myself into trouble, start to lose them, my voice too, and start wondering how I'm going to finish them. I've written a lot out of longing and grief and desire, for sure. King of Hurtin'—that's me. Anyway I end up reading few of those poems.

Reader:

What's this got to do with Black Mountain? Robert Duncan?

Writer:

I did work on him, yes. I did, and it was an exhilarating experience. He was just dazzlingly smart and he showed me a lot about what can be done in contemporary form. So did a lot of others.

Reader:

Others? Who in particular?

Writer:

Just about anybody I've ever read, it seems, at least in the short run. I was thrilled when just after I'd arrived at the University of Manitoba (in 1973 this was) Arnason told me about a bunch of writers who were sometimes called the Tish poets, and said they had been heavily influenced by some of the same writers I had been reading as a graduate student in Rochester. So I got reading them too and they had an impact, especially George Bowering. And then there were others, Doug Barbour for one. Barbour's one of the best poets and critics in Canada and he gets very little credit. Some of the earlier American poets too—William Carlos Williams, Ezra Pound, e.e. cummings. Robert Kroetsch and Eli Mandel have mattered a lot to me. Kroetsch's influence—his criticism as well as his poetry and prose fiction—is pretty obvious, I guess. Mandel had quite a different effect. I worked hard on him for several years, and I wrote a monograph and several essays on him and taught graduate courses on him. For years when people asked me about his influence I'd say no, there wasn't much, not really. And then one time when I sat down and strayed over a few Cooley titles I was struck by how much he was there. And there is Gerard Manley Hopkins—god I love him. A.R. Ammons, same thing. Well, I've not read a huge amount of his work, to tell the truth, but I love it. I tend to go for writing that is highly charged, and to take little pleasure in poetry that is abstract and essayistic. bp Nichol. Michael Ondaatje. Two of my heroes. Do you know the British poet who wrote those zany colloquial pieces—Roger McGough? Wonderful. Doug Jones. Not all these writers have greatly influenced how I go about things, but they are important to me. Al Purdy, of course. Frank Davey as a critic. When he's on he's absolutely brilliant. Andy Suknaski—I can't leave out Suknaski. There are more, always more.

Reader:

I can't help noticing that you've mentioned no women. Were female poets unimportant to you?

Writer:

Hardly unimportant: I've always read them with great pleasure and admiration. Dorothy Livesay, Denise Levertov, P.K. Page, H.D., Phyllis Webb, Anne Sexton, Margaret Atwood, Maxine Kumin, Miriam Waddington. Sharon Olds—one of my all-time favourites. Elizabeth Bishop, Rita Dove, Méira Cook. And now, recently, Anne Compton. They've been really significant to me as a reader, but other than the brief imitations I go through with almost everyone, I can't say that they have guided my writing all that much.

Reader:

You think of yourself as a prairie poet, right?

Writer:

Definitely. That's crucial to what I'm doing and why I'm doing it. In one way or another my writing is strongly connected to the prairies. So are most of my other literary activities. I was a founding member of the Manitoba Writers' Guild and a founding editor with Turnstone. I've been active in teaching prairie literature at the University, writing about it, editing and publishing it. We've held many conferences at St. John's College that have dealt in whole or in part with prairie writing and now in the fall of 2006 we are in the process of organizing our fourth major conference on the prairies. So there's that.

I'd also think of myself as a postmodern writer, though my sense of what that can mean is a bit broader than some people's, and a little sharper than others'. I don't think that dealing with a contentious issue in itself makes you postmodern, and I am a little puzzled over the willingness of readers and writers to claim the status once the term had taken on some respectability. On the other hand, I don't think that postmodernism should be defined so narrowly that it includes only the language poets. In any case, I'm concerned about how readily language poetry refuses the full resources available to a writer, including, god forbid, referentiality. Of course you can do this for yourself if you like, but why disallow its use for others?

Reader:

I guess it's because they think reference is a big problem.

Writer:

And so it is. Their arguments are powerful. I guess I'm not quite so willing to give up on it, or set it aside. My question is: because reference is uncertain, need we abandon it? I am taken by what Linda Hutcheon has to say about this. She argues that those texts and theories that resist reference become, or would seem to become, retreats from the world and exits into purely formal construction. For her, they are not instances of postmodernism at all, but examples of late modernism. In her writing about postmodernism she also points to the particular, the local, and the specific as means of resisting supposed universals. I am arguing it is the specific weight that makes the local such a crucial part of the prairie postmodern. It certainly is part of the ambitious long poem that comes out of the prairies: Barry MacKinnon, *I Wanted to Tell you Something*; Robert Kroetsch, *Seed Catalogue*; David Arnason, *Marsh Burning*; Birk Sproxton, *Headframe*; probably even Patrick Friesen, *The Shunning* (though he probably would deny any such affiliation). It is there, I think, in what Jon Whyte has done too; and probably as early as Anne Marriott's remarkable poem, *The Wind our Enemy*. It certainly informs my own long poems, such as *Bloody Jack, Fielding, Irene, country music,* and *the bentleys.*

It intrigues me that though Kroetsch is widely and admiringly read as a postmodern writer, readers from outside the prairies (especially in Ontario and British Columbia) pretty much overlook in his work and his statements a ferocious regionalism. It is as useful perhaps to think of him as a *prairie* postmodernist, which may mean a different kind of postmodernist from what you get in Vancouver or Toronto. I'd like to think that my own work in a related way draws on contemporary understandings of texts *and* roots itself in the prairie region.

Reader:

But how do you do it? What brings you into words?

Writer:

Other poets, other poets, other texts. They're crucial. I've come to be deeply suspicious of romantic notions of creation, the soul spouting like a geyser. I do believe in inspiration, strongly believe in it as a matter of fact, but I don't think an inspirational model by itself is very productive. It can also be dangerous: it can make you into a cautious writer and an intolerant reader. You know the complaints, we've all heard them. If a writer shows any signs of trying out something, anything, the predictable moans and bitchings are quick to follow: this is mannered; it is academic; it is elitist; it is inaccessible. My god, why should poetry be less demanding or more familiar than any other human activity? It can be readily accessible, of course, but why must it?

Reader:

What about your writing methods? What brings you into writing?

Writer:

Well, other writers—as I was saying. If you're asking more practically, as in when and where, at what place and hour, I'd say almost any time any where. I'm always doodling and drafting and revising and gathering notes. I love it and do it every chance I get. Invariably I am set off by my reading though. I draw on personal experiences, too, but the experiences seem often to be released into poetry, and shaped into poetry. The poems themselves—their shapes and rhythms and manner—are largely begotten by the possibilities I find in other words. I often argue that poets do not have special experiences that mark them off from others, they simply have learned how to write poems.

For me it's handy to keep my pen nearby. And I do compose largely with a pen, by the way. When I'm writing poems that is. The time it takes to write a few words gives time to happen on a few more, and the paper allows time to fill in words all over the place, which I habitually do. I get something under way and then I say: what have I got? Where might it go? What potential do I find here? About that time I enter the stuff into a computer and print it out, then have a go at the printed version and run it through endless tweakings. So I am a mad expander and reviser.

I also try to find some site around which I can write a series of related texts—Dracula poems, astronaut poems, *love in a dry land* poems, fairy tale poems, that sort of thing. Once I'm there I find I can generate material around it, and invariably I will do some research in scouting possibilities.

Reader:

So what are you doing now?

Writer:

I've got so many things on the go it's laughable. But I can identify one or two projects. I've been working for some time on a series of muse poems and metapoems which I've been calling *the muse sings*. Then there's a text built around my blown appendix, and that's gotten pretty big—the manuscript, that is; the appendix is fine. There are a set of family and Estevan poems—*correction line*. Lots more. The words pile up.

Reader:

We're about out of time, but I want to ask one last question. What about the body?

Writer:

I can't tell you how pleased I was to hear Nicole Markotić talk about the body in my writing. It's gone pretty much unnoticed up until now. Even in *Soul Searching*, which shows a lot of sympathy for the body—even there the body didn't seem to register, so that some read the book as a yearning for angels.

Editing is a thankless chore, and writing about poetry is not a whole lot more esteemed. Poets at their worst tend to be a vain and ungrateful lot, I sometimes think, at least when it comes to appreciating the kind of work that Markotić has done here. So I want to tell you I am gratified by the care and intelligence with which she—herself an exquisite poet—has assembled the book and written the introduction. Such a caring reader is what every poet dreams of finding.

—*Dennis Cooley*

Selected Cooley Poems: Sources

Leaving
Winnipeg: Turnstone Press, 1980
"A Poem for You, Leaving Winnipeg"

Fielding
Saskatoon: Thistledown Press, 1983
"*anaeurysm*"
"& we are skinbags of heated water   dreaming"

Bloody Jack (1984)
Winnipeg: Turnstone Press, 1984
"in his tangerine skin" [also in *sunfall*]
"the love song of j l krafchenko or the transcanada in (trance crypt"
"Sonya Orlowsky"

Soul Searching
Red Deer: Red Deer College Press, 1987
"Paul sd"
"Exorcism"
"I think 'Ego': Ergo I am"

Dedications
Saskatoon: Thistledown Press, 1988
"labiarinth"
"anatomy of love"

Perishable Light
Regina: Coteau Books, 1988
"prairie romance"
"behind the door"
"moon musings"

this only home
Winnipeg: Turnstone Press, 1992
"holy cow"
"inner ear"
"my eye"

Burglar of Blood
Winnipeg: Pachyderm Press, 1992
"melodious rhyme"
"he replies to his critics"
"breathless"

passwords: transmigrations between Canada and europe
Kiel, Germany: l&f Verlag, 1996
"In Germany cooley…"   "…again"
"Wished we had … just out …"   "… light rain falling"

sunfall
Concord, ON: Anansi Press, 1996
"winnipeg in winter"
"a series of shocking pre-positions

Irene
Winnipeg: Turnstone Press, 2000
"mother tongue …"
"this on remembrance weekend"
"bodies are"

Bloody Jack (2002)
Edmonton: University of Alberta Press, 2002
"jack's dictionary of cunning linguists" [expanded]

seeing red
Winnipeg: Turnstone Press, 2003
"blood brothers"
"red men ace"
"echolalia"
"the red / emption of blood"

country music
Vernon, BC: Kalamalka Press, 2004
poems with the lines beginning:
"not that he's wrong"
"a crate of apples could i suppose"
"listening to night sticky with sweat..."

lps Books in the Laurier Poetry Series
Published by Wilfrid Laurier University Press

Di Brandt *Speaking of Power: The Poetry of Di Brandt* by Di Brandt, edited by Tanis MacDonald, with an afterword by Di Brandt • 2006 • xvi + 56 pp. • ISBN-10: 0-88920-506-X; ISBN-13: 978-0-88920-506-2

Dennis Cooley *By Word of Mouth: The Poetry of Dennis Cooley* by Dennis Cooley, edited by Nicole Markotić, with an afterword by Dennis Cooley • 2007 • xxii + 62 pp. • ISBN-10: 1-55458-007-2; ISBN-13: 978-1-55458-007-1

Lorna Crozier *Before the First Word: The Poetry of Lorna Crozier* by Lorna Crozier, edited by Catherine Hunter, with an afterword by Lorna Crozier • 2005 • xviii + 62 pp. • ISBN-10: 0-88920-489-6; ISBN-13: 978-0-88920-489-8

Christopher Dewdney *Children of the Outer Dark: The Poetry of Christopher Dewdney* by Christopher Dewdney, edited by Karl E. Jirgens, with an afterword by Christopher Dewdney • 2007 • xviii + 82 pp. • ISBN-10: 0-88920-515-9; ISBN-13: 978-0-88920-515-4

Tim Lilburn *Desire Never Leaves: The Poetry of Tim Lillburn* by Tim Lilburn, edited by Alison Calder, with an afterword by Tim Lilburn • 2007 • xiv + 50 pp. • ISBN-10: 0-88920-514-0; ISBN-13: 978-0-88920-514-7

Don McKay *Field Marks: The Poetry of Don McKay* by Don McKay, edited by Méira Cook, with an afterword by Don McKay • 2006 • xxvi + 60 pp. • ISBN-10: 0-88920-494-2; ISBN-13: 978-0-88920-494-2

Al Purdy *The More Easily Kept Illusions: The Poetry of Al Purdy* by Al Purdy, edited by Robert Budde, with an afterword by Russell Brown • 2006 • xvi + 82 pp. • ISBN-10: 0-88920-490-X; ISBN-13: 978-0-88920-490-4